A LITTLE BOOK OF

ISLAM

A short guide for curious westerners

by

Patrick C. Notchtree

Published by Limebury Books

ISBN 978-0-9572361-8-9

@pcnotchtree

24/3

Contents

Acknowledgements

"Islam, the Way of Submission", by Solomon Nigosian, Toronto, Canada.

Idlan Zakaria, Kuala Lumpur, Malaysia.

Ghufar Razaq, Lerwick, Shetland Islands, Scotland

Andrew (Drew) Dalton
Senior Lecturer in Social Sciences, University of Sunderland

Foreword by Andrew Dalton

MashAllah! A little book of Islam is an excellent read. As a revert to Islam, I found this book accessible, well-researched and useful pick up, read to refresh myself on the basics of Islam as a religion. For those totally new to Islam, and who know nothing about it, then this is for you. It presents a balanced, no-nonsense approach to Islam which is suitable for a newbie, a scholar or for those with a passing interest in learning about this beautiful religion. Patrick brings Islam into the modern day with some interesting comparisons to other faiths and he rightly points out contemporary issues which Islam is facing in the modern world. This is a book to have on your shelf and Inshallah, I hope that many will read it

Andrew (Drew) Dalton

Senior Lecturer in Social Sciences, University of Sunderland

Foreword by the author

Islam is scary. Muslims are scary. Or so many westerners think, and after the recent history of terrorism carried out by Muslims in the name of Islam, one can understand it if that is all they know about approximately 1.25 billion people on the planet, or about one in six people on Earth. Many Muslims who live in western countries adhere to their traditional styles of dress which makes them more easily identifiable and because they live in communities close to their mosque, this has the effect of creating areas with a high percentage, if not a majority, of Muslims in western cities.

Islam is more than just a religion as the term is usually seen in the west by most people. It is a whole way of life and is central to a Muslim's existence. But is this scary? As hostility to Islam has grown in some western countries the effect on many Muslims has been to become more withdrawn, more defensive and in some cases, hostile in return. This is in the main due to a lack of understanding by both sides of the other. The overwhelming majority of Muslims abhor the murderous atrocities of fanatics who follow a highly extreme and minority version of Islam.

History is full of the murderous atrocities carried out by committed Christians who believe their fundamentalist belief justifies their actions; everything from the Crusades against Islam to the colonisation and enforced conversions carried out by Europeans across the world to today's persecution and even murders of LGBT people in so-called Christian countries, to give just one example.

Fear can often be explained by ignorance of the other and I hope that this little book will help in a small way to spread a little more knowledge of Islam and its followers and help to bridge a widening gap between Muslims and the societies in the west where they live.

Patrick C Notchtree

1 - Introduction

The Rt. Reverend David Jenkins, one time Bishop of Durham and perhaps the most outspoken Christian priest and theologian of his day, once said, "The trouble with Christianity is some of the Christians." Much the same could be said of most religions I suspect, but it is certainly true of Islam. The trouble with Islam is some of the Muslims.

Most people are aware of the links between Christianity and Judaism, but perhaps fewer realise that Islam is the third major religion from the same historic roots going back to Adam and Abraham.

Islam has undoubtedly had a "bad press" in recent years, and there are many varied misconceptions about it. Some terrible things have been done in the name of Islam, as they have with Christianity and other religions, but as with Christianity, this is not a true reflection of what the religion is about.

The purpose of this little book is to introduce some of the basic facts about Islam, what it is and what it is not, so that we may gain a greater understanding of the world we all share.

I am not a Muslim and make no claim to be a great expert on Islam, but some years ago I wanted for various reasons to find out more about this force which shapes the lives of about a sixth of the world's population, and therefore did some research. It was later suggested I share this knowledge with other interested people.

The word Islam is, like the religion itself, of Arabic origin, and also means submission, but with the additional meaning of peace. The Muslim therefore submits himself to the will of God, and thereby his soul finds peace.

Although Islam originated in the Arabian peninsular, it is not just an Arab religion; in fact more than half the world's Muslims are not Arabs, for Islam is predominant in a broad swathe of territory stretching from the coast of west Africa, through the Middle East, central Asia, Pakistan, India, the Far East and Indonesia (the world's most populous Muslim country), and there are Muslims in every country in the world.

As with Christianity, there are divisions within Islam, but all those have in common the belief in the one true God, Allah, and the message and primacy of His chosen human messenger to mankind, the Prophet Muhammad.

Next we will begin to explore how Islam views the nature of God, and the role of the Prophet Muhammad, whom Muslims never mention without invoking the Peace and Blessing of God.

Space for reader's notes

2 – The nature of God or Allah

At the heart of Islam is the belief in God, Allah, and Muslims are very firm in their belief of the oneness and the unity of God. This is a major source of conflict with Christianity, which many Muslims regard as a polytheistic or multi-god religion because of the Christian belief in the Trinity. More than once in the Qur'an (of which more in later chapters), the association of other entities with God is denounced in the most vehement terms. Muslims regard the association implied by the Trinity as "a monstrous sin" (Qur'an 4:51). This of course stems from a misunderstanding of the Christian Trinity, but I haven't the space to go into that one here. The veneration accorded to the Virgin Mary by some Christian churches is also deplored on the same grounds.

On the subject of sin, the worst of which is stated above, the Christian concept of original sin does not apply in Islam. Of course humans are not infallible and are naturally imperfect, but the idea that one is born with Adam's sin on one's soul is rejected. People are therefore responsible for their actions. Sin is not inherited, and is forgiven if one submits to the will of God. Adam did, and was forgiven. To advocate a faith different to Islam is to deny God and His Unity, and forfeits one's place as part of Islamic society.

God exists, has existed and will exist for all eternity. He is essential, unique, unsubstantial, unembodied, formless and omnipresent. These are the characteristics of God. He also has seven attributes, those of life, knowledge, power, will, speech, sensibility and activity. The four activities of God are creation, preservation, revelation and predestination.

As with any great religion, there have been, and are, differing schools of theology within Islam which seek to interpret these characteristics, attributes and activities, and have arrived at differing answers, beyond the scope of a short book like this.

Muslims have ninety-nine names for God which pious Muslims recite using a rosary, and will call upon God using an appropriate one when praying to Him on a particular matter. There is not space here for all ninety-nine, but examples are The Compassionate, The Merciful, The Protector, The Mighty, The Forgiver, The Eternal, The Avenger etc. The list is not regarded as a memory test, but serves to remind Muslims that God is the "Lord of all spheres and realms". Nearer to man than his neck vein, He reveals himself only as He chooses. The full list is at Appendix 1.

3 – Angels and Genie

Angels feature strongly in Islamic belief and theology. Like humans, they are also created by God but they are sexless, immortal and made of light. They are ranked above ordinary humans, but beneath the Prophets.

When the angels were commanded by God to prostrate themselves before Adam, one arrogant angel refused and so fell from grace. He is Satan (Shaitan or Iblis), the fallen angel.

Other angels have defined roles. There are four archangels, Gabriel, the angel of revelation, Michael, the angel of providence, Israfil, destined to blow the last trumpet and Izra'il, the angel of death.

There are also a large number of other Angels, some of whom surround God on His throne, some chronicle the thoughts, words and deeds of all humanity and some receive the souls of the dead.

Angels are of course familiar to Christians, but Islam also has a tradition of belief in genie called jinn. They are not angels but are mortal beings, created earlier than man from the fire of the scorching wind. (Qur'an 15:27). These live an existence parallel to man, living in communities and marrying. (If this seems impossible, consider that modern physics now regards the existence of parallel universes as inevitable so I for one reserve judgement. Is the traditional magic lamp an allegory for some kind of portal?) They are normally invisible to humans, but may appear in human form, or in another guise. They may also live in trees or even human homes. (The idea of possession by devils in Christianity along with exorcism and even ghost haunting correlates with this.) This seems to be the origin of the western idea of the genie, who is usually depicted as vaguely oriental.

Muslims regard the jinn as mainly hostile to humans, and who endeavour to bring to bear bad influences upon them. Worship of Jinn was widespread in Arabia before Islam and seems to have been integrated into the Islamic belief system at an early stage.

Modern Muslim thinkers explain the jinn as symbolising natural forces or disease, but popular belief remains that they are beings fashioned before man. Humans may be possessed by jinn, which is considered a kind of mental illness.

Having said that, poets are also in the group of those considered possessed, which led the Prophet Muhammad fervently to deny being a poet, although the Qur'an is considered perfection in Arabic. Of his central role in Islam, more in the next chapter.

4 – The Prophet Muhammad and the birth of Islam

Islam stems from the common Judaic and Christian roots, but its origins are usually taken to lie with the birth of the Prophet Muhammad in Arabia about AD 570. (570 CE).

Arabia at that time was in turmoil. It was ruled by Arab chieftains who fought each other, as well as the Persian Empire in the east, the Christian Byzantine Empire in the north and their Christian Ethiopian allies to the south and west. Religion was based around natural forces with various local gods and goddesses.

Mecca, the place of birth of Muhammad, had promoted itself as a centre of pilgrimage to the Kaaba, a large cubic shrine, containing a holy black stone. This brought trade and wealth to Mecca. The Kaaba was an ancient Arabic shrine and centre of worship for Arab tribes long before Muhammad's time, and it and its traditions, such as the Hajj or pilgrimage, were integrated into Islam in its early days. The Qur'an states this it was originally built by Ibrahim (Abraham) and Ishmael on the orders of God. The Black Stone is thought to be a meteorite, demonstrating the site's importance as the link between earth and heaven. Muhammad's wisdom and ability to settle disputes was demonstrated some years before he started to receive the revelations from God. After a renovation of the Kaaba, the various tribes could not agree who should have the honour of replacing the Black Stone. Muhammad, then aged thirty-five, asked for a cloth and, held by the various tribal representatives, this was used to transport the Black Stone to its place, with Muhammad finally placing it. All the tribes were satisfied with this solution, and Muhammad's reputation was enhanced. There is a tradition in Islam that Muhammad was descended from Abraham.

Muhammad's early life was probably spent in travel, trading around Arabia with his uncle who raised him from the age of eight, both his parents having died by then. It was through this trade that he met and married a wealthy widow, Kadijah, who was impressed by his high moral qualities. He was twenty-five and she was forty. They had six children, two sons who died in infancy and four daughters. The best known of these was Fatima, who married Muhammad's cousin Ali. Until the death of Kadijah in AD619 (619 CE), he took no other wife.

The financial security his marriage provided gave him the opening to indulge his spiritual side, and he spent much time in meditation, often going for walks in the hills to think.

About AD610 (610 CE), when he was forty, he was on such a trip when he was terrified by the appearance of the angel Gabriel saying, "Muhammad, you are God's messenger" and commanding him to recite. He did not know what to recite, and the angel answered him with verses about God. Muhammad rushed back to Kadijah convinced he was either mad or had indeed had a divine visit and a call to be a prophet. When she heard the full story, she was convinced of the latter and reassured him.

His doubts vanished when he received further revelations. He believed these came directly from God and continued until his death in AD632 (632 CE). So he became known as rasul Allah, God's Messenger, and was later ordered to declare openly this status.

These messages were written down and memorised by his followers, who after his death collected them together to form the Holy Book of Islam, the Qur'an, which survives to this day.

Muhammad's religious teachings aroused hostility from various vested interests, and after the death of Kadijah his life was threatened. The events of his later life will be described next.

Space for reader's notes

Space for reader's notes

5 – Later life of the Prophet and the spread of Islam

Muhammad, like other prophets before him - and he is regarded as the last, definitive prophet of a line that includes Jesus - saw as his mission to spread the news his revelations had brought him. There were four main themes, the oneness of God, the power and goodness of God, the responsibility of man towards God and the judgement awaiting mankind on the day of resurrection. As he preached the worship of a single God, his following grew. His movement took the name Islam and his followers were called Muslims. In the Qur'an though, they are called "the Believers".

It is important to note that while Muslims recognise Jesus as a prophet, and a very important one, he is simply that, a prophet. To attach divinity to Jesus is regarded as sinful because only God is divine. Muhammad himself is never regarded as divine but simply human, having the special status of being the final prophet bringing the ultimate message of God, therefore being known as the Seal of the Prophets.

His preaching inferred disapproval of the lifestyle of the wealthy, who tried to bribe him. Muhammad rejected this absolutely. His attack on the traditional religions, most of which involved multiple gods and centred on the Kaaba, alienated him from the powerful in Mecca who felt threatened by his growing popularity. As a result, Muhammad and his followers faced economic, personal and physical persecution. At about this time, he received assurances of his safety in Medina, so the Muslims left Mecca and were followed soon by Muhammad, who escaped just in time to avoid being murdered. His knowledge of the hill country enabled him to arrive safely in Medina on 24 September, 622 (622 CE).

This escape is known as the Hijrah, sometimes rendered in English as Hegira. All Islamic calendars date from this and are known as AH, Anno Hegira, in the Latin form. The Hijrah is regarded as a turning point both in the development of Islam and in world history.

The Medinans soon became converts to Islam, and Muhammad's status as arbiter of disputes was established.

Trade disputes though soon involved the Medinans in a long war with Mecca, in which Muhammad was actively involved in pursuit of spreading Islam. Although he suffered reverses and was injured in one battle, his stature grew as his successes led to more converts and increased wealth.

Later he achieved his ambition of conquering Mecca and bringing it into Islam, achieving this with very little loss of life. He was now the most powerful ruler in Arabia. He was planning a raid into Syria when he fell ill and died, leaving no instructions about a successor and Islam in crisis. This led to the greatest schism in Islam, of which more in a later chapter.

Muhammad is revered for his piety, spiritual leadership and both his political and military skills. In Islam he built a movement with a remarkable bond of faith and sense of brotherhood.

Space for reader's notes

Space for reader's notes

6 – The Qur'an

Muslims believe that God, or Allah, chose the Prophet Muhammad to give to mankind His revelation and His message. This was given to Muhammad and this verification of God's word is recorded in the Qur'an, the Holy Book of Islam. As Muslims believe that the Qur'an is the word of God, it is essential to Islam and the way in which Muslims are to live their lives. As a Muslim child grows up, an important part of education is the learning of Qur'anic texts. Suitable passages are used for marriage ceremonies and to provide comfort in misfortune.

Muslims view the Qur'an as more than this though. It is the conclusion and climax of all earlier Holy Scriptures. It accordingly provides direction on every aspect of life, both in personal and public life. It is the ultimate and infallible word of God, through Muhammad, to mankind. Four other books are viewed as Holy Scripture by Muslims, these being The Scrolls, revealed to the Prophet Abraham and now lost, The Torah, revealed to the Prophet Moses, The Psalms, revealed to the Prophet David and The Gospels, the revelation of Jesus Christ, seen by Muslims as a prophet, but not divine. Not even Muhammad was divine, he was very human as we have seen, but a standard for men to follow.

The message of God was sent to Muhammad to correct the errors of the earlier revelations produced by man's imperfections.

The Qur'an was given to Muhammad in Arabic, and this gives that language divine status as God's chosen instrument of revelation. Translations of the Qur'an are therefore frowned upon as corruptions of God's Holy Message. Muslim scholars dispute whether a translation can express the Word of God. The literary style of the Qur'an is regarded as perfection in Arabic. It was gathered together in the twenty-five years after Muhammad's death which makes it perhaps the most contemporaneous Holy Scripture on the planet.

Gabriel's first command to Muhammad was, "Recite!", and Muslims have obeyed this divine command ever since and recitation of the Qur'an is an important part of Islamic worship and ritual.

There is more about this in the next chapter.

Space for reader's notes

7 – The Qur'an 2

The Qur'an means literally, "Recitation", and for Muslims, the recitation of the Qur'an is essential to their faith. Quiet belief is not enough. In the Qur'an itself there are a number of exhortations to recite, indicating the true Muslim.

Both Jewish and Christian scriptures are collections of works from various sources; the Qur'an is remarkable among scriptures in that it is all the revelation of God, or Allah, through one man. Its subject matter is human life and offers direction to mankind on how to accept God through following the "straight" path. The dignity and foolishness of mankind, Judgement Day and the reality of God's mercy are the dominating themes.

Muhammad never learned to read and write. Literacy as we understand it today was unusual then and was normally the preserve of specialist scribes. The revelations of God given to Muhammad were noted by some of his followers who were scribes. After Muhammad's death the Qur'an was compiled by these scribes. This led to a number of different versions with slight variations. These were later standardised by Uthman (also known as Osman) who was a contemporary adherent of Muhammad and later succeeded him as Caliph. Caliph means successor or deputy and leaders of Islam after Muhammad adopted this title.

Non-Muslim theologians have attempted to analyse the sources of the Qur'an in terms of Jewish and Christian roots, along with Arabic influences. While some claim to have found threads, there are considerable difficulties in this.

Of course, Muslims would expect this because they believe that the Qur'an is the authentic word of God, and that to look for its roots in human history is not just pointless but also blasphemous.

The move towards Judgement Day, the lure of paradise and the dread of hell are clearly described because the morality of mankind is God's concern. The contradictions of human nature cause tension and conflict both within and between men. It follows that social and economic justice will be gained from human moral order.

To achieve this, the Qur'an prescribes five duties, the Five Pillars of Islam, which are the confession of faith, daily prayer, the giving of alms, fasting and pilgrimage. These are discussed in more detail in later chapters.

The Qur'an is stringent in its demands for obedience to its teaching, it also emphasises the infinite mercy of God.

The Qur'an illustrates God's concern in the betterment of human beings with historical illustrations, which show that although mankind can be extremely obstinate and foolish, there exists within us all remarkable potential and the strength to overcome all evil.

The Will of God is the source of this strength, and although all have its potential, selected humans have been endowed with this in such strength that they are required to pronounce God's word and so shape the future of mankind.

Such humans are the prophets, and Muhammad is the final prophet, and the Qur'an the final and definitive message of God to mankind.

The teaching of the Qur'an continues.

Space for reader's notes

Space for reader's notes

8 - The teaching of the Qur'an

Muslims believe the Qur'an is the final and definitive message of God to mankind. Some who are particularly staunch adherents are therefore not prepared to compromise Islamic principles.

The concept of Jihad or Holy War is one that causes great concern in the West. Of course, claiming that one's cause in war is holy and just is not confined to Islam. Many wars have been fought with both sides claiming divine approval. Yet the motivating force driving Islam is the bringing of God's peace to mankind, but Islam more than other religions is prepared to approve aggression in order to achieve this end. The Muslim, by partaking in struggle against all that is counter to the truth of God, finds peace and harmony. Do the ends justify the means? This is an age-old argument, and one not confined to Islam, or even to religion.

The Qur'an promises those killed or defeated in Jihad will be rewarded by God. Militants construe this as a call to subjugate non-Islamic parts of the world to the true religion, but most others in the modern world see it as a call to struggle against evil within man.

The Qur'an prescribes other codes of conduct also. Alcohol and gambling are prohibited as "works of the devil"

(5:93). Polygamy is allowed up to a maximum of four wives, but only if the husband can look after them. Many Muslims follow the model of the Prophet and have only one wife. Marriage is seen as a purely civil contract, with no sacramental significance. Therefore divorce is permitted under certain circumstances.

Sexual relations outside marriage are forbidden, (except with slaves), and incest is absolutely forbidden. Inheritance laws grant males twice as much as females, to take into consideration their greater responsibilities.

There are protracted sections in the Qur'an which deal with such things as the care and honour of parents, murder and revenge, property rights, usury and more.

Integrity, humility and kindness are cited as virtues and attitudes that should rule everyday living.

At the time when Islam was born, slavery was an accepted part of the structure of society. The Qur'an makes several references to slavery, emphasising the slave's equality in religious terms while recognising the slave's inferior status in other ways. Muslims are urged to be kind to their slaves, to allow them to earn their freedom or even to grant it as an act of kindness. Many slaves occupied high positions in later Muslim society, some exercising power and wealth. The use of female slaves as prostitutes through force is condemned in the Qur'an.

The reverence in which the Qur'an is held is difficult for non Muslims to comprehend. In some countries, children as young as ten are required to memorise the whole book, all 6,239 verses or 77,934 words. This can create problems when such children are temporarily at school in non-Islamic countries, and they are often absent to keep up with Islamic studies and with others of their age back home. All Muslim children must learn selected parts of the Qur'an.

Adult Muslims often quote appropriate parts of the Qur'an before beginning a particular task. Many carry a copy all the time.

A much-loved quote is, "Covet not that which God has bestowed on some of you in preference to others" (4:36) and the poor, especially beggars, are apt to quote, "Good deeds drive away evil deeds" (11:116).

To the Muslim the Qur'an is God's Word, sent by Allah via Gabriel to Muhammad; it is incomparable, matchless and of universal relevance.

Space for reader's notes

Space for reader's notes

9 – Tradition and Hadith

After the Qur'an, Muslims look to two other sources of inspiration. The Hadith, which means "narrative", and includes the Sunnah, and which taken together are the tradition of actions and sayings of the Prophet Muhammad and his followers. There is an immense amount of this material, but unlike the Qur'an, which is regarded as the Word of God, Muslims disagree over the Hadith and what should or should not be included. No definitive Hadith has ever been recognized. Nevertheless, the importance of this is that it is an important resource of the teachings of Muhammad and the early Muslims who knew him well.

To be included, each entry must be verified by setting out the chain of those who have passed it on from the person who transcribed it right back to the Prophet or one of his close companions. The Hadith, unlike the Qur'an which was written down more or less at the time, it contains a high degree of oral tradition, but nonetheless is of importance for the insight it gives to the teachings of the Prophet. These ideas and values are therefore identified as Islamic, and have been of great weight in shaping Islamic Law.

In order to verify the Hadith, enormous volumes of biography have been built up by Muslim scholars over the centuries about the narrators of Hadith. Some compilations are given more credence than others. Different sects within Islam recognize differing selections of Hadith, the Sunnis some parts, the Shi'ites others. Later splits led to other selections, for example the shorter one of the Sufis.

In spite of all its imperfections, the Hadith is a vital human link for Muslims going right back to the Prophet and his followers.

The Hadith contains stories about the life and principles held by the Prophet Muhammad, and Muslims all over the world have modelled their lives on his; eating as he ate, washing as he washed and living their lives in every way possible as he did. To staunch Muslims, the Prophet is a very real part of their daily lives, and his influence comes just as much from the tradition of the Hadith as from the teachings of the Holy Qur'an.

Fasting on Mondays and Thursdays is not called for in the Quran. However, it is encouraged to do so because the Prophet Muhammad did that; it's part of the Sunnah which basically means 'the way of life of the Prophet' , which Muslims are encouraged to follow. Another thing is that it is also encouraged to fast on every alternate day, as this is believed to be what was done by King David, revered in Islam not just for slaying Goliath but for receiving the Psalms and is known in Islam as the Prophet Daud, the Arabic form of the name.

10 – Expansion and Decline

There is a special place in Islam for the "People of the Book"; those who believe in God, revelation and the Scriptures, that is to say the other Abrahamic religions, the Jews and Christians, upon which the Prophet insisted. He was therefore able to guarantee tolerance in the early Islamic community, thereby enabling expansion. The final years of the Prophet's life were devoted to consolidating Islam, but his sudden and unexpected death in AD 632 (632 CE) left Islam in crisis. A political heir was vital, but of course there was no question of a religious heir. Muhammad was the final and greatest, the "seal" of the prophets, and no further word was needed.

Muhammad's father-in- law was elected the first Caliph. The Caliph is both the political and religious leader of Islam and is the successor to the Prophet himself. The Caliphate was passed down through successive dynasties, the most famous of which is the Abbasids, who held it from 750 to 1517 when the Ottoman Turks conquered Egypt where the Caliphate was by that time based. From then the Ottoman Sultan held the office, right up to 1924 when Kemal Atatürk abolished it during his modernisation of Turkey after the Ottoman Empire's collapse after the first world war.

The first Caliphs had the task of suppressing the divisions that the untimely death of the Prophet brought about, and this gave rise to schisms within Islam that survive to this day. These will be dealt with in a later chapter. The machinations, manoeuvrings and internal strife among the early aspirants for the Caliphate is a remarkable story, and makes intriguing reading.

The military expertise that had been developed led to the swift expansion of Islam from Arabia into Egypt and north Africa, and east into what is now Iraq and Iran.

Some of these early Caliphs were outstanding men, with great talent not only for military leadership, but civil administration, learning and legal matters. If rival Caliphates were set up, they were crushed, and Islam expanded yet further. In AD 691 (691 CE) the glorious and iconic Dome of the Rock mosque was built in Jerusalem by Abd-al-Malik. By 710, Islam spread across the Straits of Gibraltar, across Spain extending as far as southern France. This progress was finally stopped at Tours in 732. To the east also conquest was as impressive, through India and as far as China. The only major block to Islamic expansion was into eastern Europe by the then strong Byzantine Empire based at Constantinople, modern Istanbul. This was not all plain sailing and there were periods of great chaos, but there was also great art and culture, such as the founding of Cairo University in 970 and the 1653 building of the Taj Mahal in India. The defeat of the Byzantine Empire in 1071 took Islam to the gates of Constantinople. Byzantium asked Christendom for aid, which led to a series of Crusades which were initially successful. It wasn't until 1492 that Islam was finally driven out of its last footholds in Spain after seven hundred years. The legacy of this can be seen today especially in southern Spain with some spectacular Islamic architecture. But Islam was not in decline and within decades the Ottoman Turks, now the leading power in Islam, had conquered the Balkans and were at the gates of Vienna. The legacy of this Balkan conquest is a European Muslim population and its effects are with us today and led to the terrible conflicts there of the late twentieth century. This was the height of the Muslim Empire, which had become coupled to the fate of the Ottoman Turkish Empire. This great empire gradually declined until it joined into the First World War on the side of the Kaiser's Germany. This led to the Arab revolt against the Turks (in which the British Colonel T.E. Lawrence, "Lawrence of Arabia", played an important part) and allied invasion which in turn led to final defeat of the Ottomans. Their empire was divided up among the victors. The crass way in which this was done without regard for local differences and allegiances, not least religious differences within Islam, has led directly to many of the troubles in the middle east a century later.

Turkey, what was left of the vast empire, underwent radical change and the Caliphate was formally abolished in 1924.

A short book like this cannot do justice to the many and varied achievements of the Islamic empire. While emphasis here has been mainly on military and religious expansion, Islam brought great art and culture, spectacular engineering and mathematical progress to the world.

Space for reader's notes

11 – Sunnis, Shi'ites and other divisions

Like most other religions, Islam has its divisions. As Christianity has three main strands, Protestant, Catholic and Orthodox, Islam has three main ones also, Sunni, Shi'ite and Sufi.

These schisms go back into the history of Islam, but it is worth noting that there is normally a strong bond among Muslims, no matter which sect they are in. There are exceptions of course, notably the militants such as Daesh or Islamic State whose extreme interpretation of Islam leads them to commit atrocities not just against non-Muslims but also Muslims of other sects.

The problems started with the death of the Prophet Muhammad. Some said that Muhammad had nominated his cousin Ali to succeed him, while others said he left no directives and thus they could elect a new leader. The second group prevailed while Ali's group accepted this for the sake of unity.

But restlessness followed and the third elected Caliph, Uthman (sometimes rendered as Osman), was assassinated in AD 656 (656 CE). Ali's supporters seized their opportunity and proclaimed him the fourth Caliph. This led to the permanent division of Islam. Ali's supporters were the legitimists or Shi'ites, opposed to the traditionalists, or Sunni. Subsequent years were ones of chaos and led to further divisions, few of which continue to exist today. But the enmity and slaughter between the majority Sunni and the Shi'ites, especially the murder at Karbala in modern Iraq of the Shi'ite Hussein, who was the Prophet's grandson, has continued since, and still gives rise to conflict today, as in the Iran/Iraq war of the 1980s and within Iraq and across the middle east today. Shi'ite "passion plays" still commemorate the martyrdom of Hussein. Such religious wounds run deep; one only has to think of the persecutions of Catholics by protestants and the persecutions of protestants by Catholics (think of the Inquisition) – all supposed to be Christians.

Early on the political differences between the Sunnis and Shi'ites took on a religious dimension too. The Sunnis believe in the idea of the consensus or ijma whereas Shi'ites, as supporters of Ali and his successors, view the Imam as the personification of Islam, and the pronouncements of the Imam as coming from Allah and therefore beyond questioning. They regard the Imams as divinely chosen to lead Muslims and that they are incapable of error. Shi'ites also have some different practices of worship and pilgrimage. For many Shi'ites the pilgrimage to Karbala, the shrine of Hussein, is as important as the pilgrimage to Mecca.

The Shi'ite belief is the official religion of Iran and has been for a long time, and there are Shi'ites in Iraq, India and many other places round the world. There are divisions within the Shi'ites, perhaps the best known are the Druze of Lebanon, a small but zealous group of about 200,000 who forbid inter-marriage.

Sunnis form the vast majority within Islam, who follow the teachings of the Prophet but are less bothered about who is or is not descended from Muhammad. Their primary precept is that of majority consensus, while maintaining tolerance of other strands within Islam. They do not believe in the infallibility of Imams and disagree with the Shi'ites in other ways too. Today, 90% of the world's Muslims are Sunni.

The Sufi are a spiritual sect based in asceticism going back to the days of the Islamic Empire. They try to attain as great a closeness to God as possible, sometimes to the exclusion of all else. The "whirling dervishes" were a group within Sufism trying to attain this godly ecstasy. The Sufis have been huge missionaries for Islam and have carried out many public services, and can in some ways be compared to Christian monasticism. The growth of fundamentalism in the recent decades has seen a decline in the influence of Sufism.

This is just an overview of the groups within Islam, and inevitably contains generalisations. There are more sub-divisions than can be described in a short book such as this.

Space for reader's notes

12 – Sharia

Islamic law, the Sharia, lays down the morality of the Islamic community. In an Islamic society it can be seen that the term law has a broader meaning than it does in the modern secular West, because Islamic law embraces both legal and moral imperatives. For this reason, not all Islamic law is set out as legal rules or is enforceable by the courts. Much of it depends solely on conscience.

Islamic law is derived from four sources, or "roots of law." The first two are the written sources, the Qur'an and the Sunna, or Hadith. The third is called ijtihad ("responsible individual opinion"). It may be used when a problem is not covered by the Qur'an or Hadith; a jurist may then determine it by using analogical reasoning (qiyas). This was first used when Islamic theologians and jurists in subjugated territories were faced with the need to assimilate local customs and laws with the Qur'an and Hadith. Later, Islamic powers-that-be considered this original thinking a threat to the Qur'an and Hadith and laid down strict rules governing its use. Because of the changes in the Muslim world community during the last few decades, however, a new importance has been attached to the innovative thinking of ijtihad.

The fourth source is the consensus (ijma) of the community, which is reached by gradually abandoning some opinions and accepting others. Because Islam has no official doctrinaire authority like a Pope or Patriarch, this is an informal process that often takes a long period of time.

Five schools of law arose in Islam, four Sunni and one Shi'ite. The four Sunni schools came about in the first two hundred years of Islam: the Shafi'i, the Hanafi, the Maliki, and the Hanbali. These use systematic reasoning to decide areas of law not covered by the Qur'an or Hadith. They differ chiefly in their stress on documentary authority or analogical reasoning, but each school recognizes the decisions of the others as being entirely legitimate and within the structure of orthodox Islam. Each school tends to be predominant in geographical areas: the Hanbali in Saudi Arabia; the Maliki in North Africa; the Shafi'i in Southeast Asia; and the Hanafi in the Indian subcontinent, central Asia, Turkey, and to some extent in Egypt, Jordan, Syria, Iraq, and Palestine. The Shi'ite school (called the Imami) dominates in Iran. This last school rejects the process of qiyas and assigns to the Imam absolute authority on matters religious, political and legal.

13 – The Sharia, social and family relationships

Islamic Law or Sharia dictates all aspects of life, religious, social and political. It includes matters of personal hygiene, how to greet people, many customs and good manners. The Sharia law sets out man's relationship and duties to God, Allah, and also man's relationship and duties to his fellow man.

The early Islamic community emphasised strengthening the family at the expense of old tribal loyalties, although it was not able to stifle these. The Qur'an emphasizes "love and mercy" between husband and wife. Men and women are confirmed as equal, "except that men are a degree higher" because they are given the duty of managing the household spending. Sexual fidelity is firmly demanded, and proven adultery is liable to be punished by 100 lashes.

The Qur'an advocates measures that were proposed to better the condition of women. The murder of baby girls, formerly common in certain tribes, is prohibited; daughters are allotted a share of inheritances, but only half of that allotted to sons because of the greater responsibilities carried by men. The Qur'an frequently stresses the kind treatment of women and grants wives the right of divorce in cases of ill-treatment.

The Qur'an sanctions polygamy, allowing up to four wives, but also states, "if you fear you cannot do justice among co-wives, then marry only one wife." Many Muslims follow the example of the Prophet and have just one wife. The exploitation of polygamy and of the husband's prerogative in traditional Islam to renounce his wife, even if she is faultless, has led in recent years to the introduction of reformed family laws in most Muslim countries.

Children's legal status depends on their legitimacy. Children conceived in marriage are under the father's care and custody, but illegitimate children's only legal relationship is with the mother. In the case of divorce or separation, custody of children goes to their mother.

Being the guardian with care and custody of children means looking after their maintenance, having control over their education, the right to contract daughters in marriage whether as children or as adults It also confers rights of succession and inheritance.

More about the Islamic approach to legal matters are covered in the next chapter.

Space for reader's notes

14 - Islamic Law; inheritance, business and the 'civil law'

The two main divisions of Islam, Sunni and Shi'ite have strikingly different inheritance systems.

Sunni laws of inheritance are based strictly on the male line of descent with a small number of females and some males not directly descended receiving a given proportion.

By contrast, the Shi'ite inheritance takes in both paternal and maternal relatives in three paths, direct descent from parents, then grandparents, sibling and their children, uncles and aunts and their children. Within each grouping, the closer the relationship, the stronger the claim; more distant relationships have a weaker claim. A full genetic relationship takes priority over a half genetic relationship.

It is worth remembering at this point that a major cause of the rift between Sunni and Shia was on exactly this issue of inheritance and succession to the Prophet Muhammad. It is therefore hardly surprising that the two sects have different inheritance systems.

In both systems however, males inherit twice the share of the female to have regard for his greater family responsibilities, and the ability of any one individual to bequeath his assets as he wishes is restricted to a third of the estate. The remainder must be distributed by the rules of inheritance.

Most people may have heard that Muslims are forbidden to charge or pay interest on financial loans. Such transactions are ruled by the prohibition of usury. In addition people who are prescribed as lacking "prudent judgement", rashid, may not manage their affairs without the permission of a guardian. These may be people who are immature or have a mental disability.

Business is carried out under four broad areas; sale, hire, gratuitous loans and gifts. There is a fifth area, exclusive to Islam which is the charitable endowment by which a person bequeaths the ownership of land to God, and the income from it is devoted forever to a religious or charitable cause. The law permits a certain percentage of such settlements to be made to the owner's family.

But the sections of Islamic Law which most people in the west hear about is not what westerners would think of as the "civil law" as has just been described, but the penal code, and this is looked at in the next chapter.

Space for reader's notes

15 – Sharia Penal Code and Punishments

In the west, most people's view of Sharia Law is centred on the Islamic Penal Code because of its perceived severity, or even barbarity. The punishment for many offences are specifically laid down in Islamic Law, but courts often use their discretion. Apostasy (renouncing Islam) and highway robbery attract the death penalty, for theft the set penalty is amputation of one or both hands, for murder and assault it may be by retaliation or compensation. Sex outside marriage by an unmarried male gets him 100 lashes but for a married male or virgin female the penalty is death. This harshness is counterbalanced because people who make false accusations earn themselves eighty lashes. Eighty lashes is also the punishment for drinking alcohol. The eating of pork is also outlawed.

The usual format of a criminal legal trial was for a single judge, qadi, to determine the guilt of the accused and then supervise the punishment. If particularly difficult legal complications arose, the counsel of a professional jurist, mufti, would be sought. Because courts had no structure in terms of lower and upper courts, the convicted person had nowhere to lodge an appeal.

Western legal systems have had significant influence in the Islamic world. In some countries a formal system of state courts have been set up, such as Egypt, Turkey and Tunisia. In others, such as Syria, Islamic Law was kept but with major modifications. Some countries continue to operate traditional Sharia Islamic Law. This is because they regard it as coming directly from Allah and is therefore divinely sanctioned and is inviolate. The sway of this thinking is increasing as more countries spurn western values which they see as un-Islamic and corrupting. Western ideas are so very different to the way that many Muslims around the world think and live, and so the traditionalists increase their influence. It is often viewed too as a fight back against what they see as colonialism, either by actual military intervention or by economic power and control. The most extreme recent example was of course the rise of Daesh or the so-called Islamic State. It must be said that vast majority of Muslims reject such extremism.

Islamic Law came from Islamic custom and was in concord with the way ordinary Muslims think. The idea of reform of the law creates conflict because it is Allah and not man who lays down the law. This conflict is evident around the Islamic world, either where western legal systems now operate and so fundamentalists seek to return to Islamic Law, or in countries that have kept Sharia law or gone back to it where people more in tune with western values fight against what they see as an oppressive and archaic system. Sometimes the backlash can be extreme, as in the case of Daesh.

Modern technology and the rapid spread of information (and disinformation) around the world through the internet etc. which is mainly western led is a problem for the fundamentalists, leading to attempts to suppress this and even trying to isolate their regimes from what they see as the corruption of the western world. Only time will tell how this conflict will be resolved.

Space for reader's notes

Space for reader's notes

16 - The Five Pillars of Islam, 1 and 2

Central to the Islamic faith are the "Five Pillars of Islam", the five duties of every Muslim. These five duties are central to Islamic life. In this chapter, two will be described.

Profession of Faith

Because of Islam's absolute commitment to belief in a single God, the first duty is the profession of faith (the Shahadah): "There is no God but Allah and Muhammad is his Prophet." This fundamental profession of faith must be made in public by every Muslim at least once in his or her lifetime, "by the tongue and with full assent from the heart"; it commits a person to their membership of the Islamic community.

Prayer

The second duty is that of five daily prayers. The first prayer is said before dawn, the second in the early afternoon, the third in the late afternoon, the fourth straight after sunset, and the fifth before going to bed and before midnight. When praying, Muslims face towards the Kaaba, the large, cube-shaped structure in the courtyard of al-Haram (the "inviolate place"), the great mosque of Mecca, described in an earlier chapter. A single unit of prayer starts with standing, then a genuflection followed by two prostrations usually kneeling with the forehead to the floor, and finally sitting. In each of these positions set prayers and portions of the Qur'an are recited.

All five prayers in Islam are communal and said in a mosque, but they may be said alone if for some reason a person cannot be present with a mosque congregation. Individual prayers are not compulsory, but Muslims are encouraged to say them after midnight; they are called tahajjud ("night-vigil"). In the Middle East and Indonesia, women also join the communal prayers, but they pray in a separate room or hall. In the Indian subcontinent, Muslim women pray at home. Before praying Muslims must carry out a ritual washing so as to be clean before Allah..

Before every prayer time at the mosque, a public call to prayer is made from a minaret or tower of the mosque by the muezzin. Traditionally this was unassisted but these days the call is often made using an amplifier so the faithful who are at some distance can still hear it.

Fridays are special in Islam. Afternoon prayers are offered on Fridays in mosques. There is a sermon first from the pulpit by the imam, known as the Khatib. Twice a year there are special religious festivals called Id. One marks the end of Ramadan during which Muslims will have observed the fasting, and the other comes after the pilgrimage to Mecca. At Id there are special prayers and sermons held in the morning. These prayers usually said outside the   mosque.

The Five Pillars of Islam are continued in the next chapter.

Space for reader's notes

Space for reader's notes

17 - The Five Pillars of Islam, 3 and 4

In the previous chapter, the first two of the Five Pillars of Islam, the Profession of Faith and that of Prayer, were discussed. In this chapter, the second two, the giving of alms and the duty of fasting are described.

Almsgiving

The third principal duty of a Muslim is to pay zakat. This was originally the tax levied by Muhammad (and later by Muslim states) on the prosperous members of society, chiefly to help the poor. It was also used for the ransom of war captives; for helping people struggling with long term debt; attracting converts to Islam and for jihad (the fight for the cause of Islam, or holy war), which, according to the Qur'an commentators, includes such things health care, education, travel and communications.

A Muslim's own property is only considered truly his and legitimate once zakat has been paid. Generally speaking these days it is no longer a government tax but is a voluntary charity, but it is still accepted as a necessary duty for all Muslims.

In some countries there has been pressure to bring it back as a government tax, but this would mean a wholesale revision of its configuration to bring it into line with the needs of a modern state.

Fasting

The fourth duty is that of fasting during the holy month of Ramadan. The Islamic calendar is lunar, that is, instead of being based of the Earth's orbit round the sun as the western calendar is, it is based on the orbit of the moon around the Earth. Because of this the months move through the western solar year. So sometimes Ramadan might fall in the summer months but it will gradually regress through the year and later would be in the winter. This did not matter much in the early days of Islam in its Arabian origins, but it can cause some difficulties these days for Muslims living in more temperate climates.

Even during hot summers, most Muslims scrupulously observe fasting. During Ramadan, one must refrain from eating, drinking, smoking, and sexual intercourse from sunrise until sunset. These activities may only take place during the hours of darkness. Of course the further north or south one lives, the variation in the seasons in the length of the day becomes more marked. In the extreme case of those north of the Arctic circle or south of the Antarctic circle, compliance would obviously be impossible because there are either months of daylight or months of darkness. Here the common sense approach and discretion must be applied and the fast observed as closely as practical. Such extreme circumstances are of course rare.

However in at least one case, western governments have voiced concern about the operation of machinery and driving by Muslims after long hours without food or drink on long midsummer days.

During Ramadan the Muslim must refrain from all sinful thoughts and actions. If they can afford to do so they should also provide food for at least one poor person. If a Muslim is ill or travelling and is suffering hardship, the Muslim need not observe the fast but has to make up for it by fasting on following days.

Space for reader's notes

Space for reader's notes

18 - The Five Pillars of Islam, 5 Pilgrimage to the Kaaba.

Muslims regard the Kaaba to be the most sacred place on earth. Muslim tradition is that Abraham and Ishmael built the holy place using foundations first laid by Adam.

In this chapter, the final of the Five Pillars of Islam, that of the Pilgrimage to Mecca, is described.

Pilgrimage

The fifth duty of the Five Pillars of Islam is the pilgrimage to the Kaaba at Mecca, the Hajj. Every Muslim who is able to do so must make this pilgrimage at least once in his or her lifetime. This takes place during the first ten days of the last month of the Islamic year. The pilgrims must enter into a state of purity symbolized by the wearing of only a seamless white garment, they must not shed blood or cut hair or nails, and they must refrain from any kind of vulgar speech or behaviour. The main parts of this long ritual are seven circuits of the Kaaba, walking fast between two mounds nearby seven times, walking the three miles to Mina, after which they walk another six miles to Arafat, staying the afternoon for a sermon there, then walking back to Mecca to offer a sacrifice commemorating Abraham's attempted sacrifice of his son Isaac, and then once more walking the circuit around the Kaaba.

These days, air travel allows Muslims from all over the world to make the Hajj. Specialist tour companies in almost every country now operate package deals to take Muslims to Mecca. Mecca is of course in modern Saudi Arabia and the increasing numbers have created problems for the Saudi authorities and there have been some instances of crushing and deaths caused by the huge numbers of Muslims attending the Hajj. The numbers are now in excess of 2 million which creates huge logistical problems for the Saudis. Through the centuries, the Kaaba has been an important meeting place for Islamic scholars for the exchange of ideas. More recently, the pilgrimage has also been used as a means for promoting political solidarity in the Muslim world.

Space for reader's notes

19 – Other duties; circumcision, sexual conduct and diet.

Of course, the duties of a Muslim do not end with the Five Pillars of Islam, described in the previous three chapters. There are other observances to be undertaken. There are many festivals, many of which are local and observed only in a particular region or country. There are however, five festivals that are observed almost universally in Islam. These are the Feast of Azha, the Feast of Fitr, the Feast of Muharram, the Birthday of the Prophet Muhammad and the Ascension or Nocturnal Journey of the Prophet Muhammad.

There are also four important observances tied to four major events in a Muslim's life; birth, circumcision, marriage and death. When the baby is a week old, he or she is named, its hair cut and the sacrifice of an animal is made in gratitude to God. The animal's meat is then given to the poor. The infant's hair is weighed, and money is distributed to the poor depending on the weight. It's usual of course to have a family gathering and a party to celebrate.

Circumcision goes back way before Islam of course and its origins are lost in the dim past. It may have had a religious significance, but the most usual reason given for circumcision of a male is hygiene, especially in a dry desert climate. It was also practised among Australian aboriginal people so it is not even a specifically Abrahamic religious custom. Male and female circumcision was the convention in Arabia before Islam, and while it is not mentioned in the Qur'an, it is in the Hadith and Law Books. Some Islamic Schools (see chapter 12) view both male and female circumcision as compulsory, others as simply as a tradition. Male circumcision is however universal in Islam. This is normally done between the age of seven to thirteen, and is again the opportunity for a family party to celebrate another step on the boy's road to manhood. Some health and hygiene benefits have been shown in the past especially in desert climates, but modern hygiene has rendered these irrelevant as a reason for male circumcision.

Female circumcision is much more controversial and is now much less common, but is still done in some parts of the Islamic world. It is often referred to now as Female Genital Mutilation (FGM). This can cause severe pain and significant long-term psychological and physical problems. No health or hygiene benefits have yet been identified. Female genital mutilation may involve the removal of the clitoris, inner and outer lips of the vagina, and the sewing or stapling together of the two sides of the vulva leaving only a small hole to pass urine and menstruate – depending on the type. Typically FGM is performed with a razor blade on girls between the ages of four and 12, traditionally without anaesthetic. In Islamic communities in western countries, it is rare and very much frowned upon by the larger society, although in some cases where the family comes from a place where it is still carried out, it may still happen. Young girls may be taken from the west back to the family's country of origin, ostensibly for a family holiday, for this to be performed, There have been cases where the girl was not informed of what was intended until it was too late. Many western countries now have or are considering laws to prohibit female circumcision.

Marriage is fundamental to Islam as the family is the nucleus of Islamic social structure. Celibacy is unusual for this reason. Also because of this, the idea of celibate monks and priests has little role in Islam. Some Sufis maintain celibacy as a route to greater godliness. (See chapter 11.) However, most Islamic thinking regards marriage as an endorsed channel for physical, emotional, social and spiritual satisfaction. Chastity outside marriage is a primary virtue, and the Qur'an recommends early marriage to remove the temptation to extra-marital sexual activity. The Qur'an absolutely forbids extra-marital affairs. While polygamy is permitted, with up to four wives provided all can be treated fairly, equally and maintained, it is now rare and most Muslim men follow the Prophet Muhammad and have one wife. Polyandry, a form of polygamy in which a woman has more than one husband, is forbidden.

Homosexuality has always been frowned upon in Islam but for long periods was tolerated and not punished. Recent decades have seen a hardening of attitudes to LGBT people, largely due to 'Christian' colonisers, and in many extreme cases leading to LGBT people being put to death.

Westerners looking at Muslims living in their communities notice the special Islamic dietary rules, especially Halal meat. In fact the term Halal is not restricted to meat, or even diet, but simply means that which is permitted as against Haram which denotes those things that are forbidden. In truth, this is not a binary, 'yes-no' situation as there are stages between the two, namely: mandatory, recommended, neutral, reprehensible, and forbidden. Some fundamentalists in recent years have tried to simplify this in order to make the differences between the west and Islam more marked. The most controversial aspect to westerners is the method of slaughter of an animal so that its meat is Halal. Contrary to western belief, these rules are devised to be as humane as possible, even if they are not always adhered to. There are variations in Islam but in essence the animal must be slaughtered quickly with a very sharp knife. The name of Allah should be invoked as this is done because all life is sacred and the recitation gives legitimacy to the taking of it by the law of necessity. The animal should not get sight of the knife beforehand, neither must it see or smell the blood from a previous slaughter which would alarm and frighten the animal. All blood must then be quickly drained from the animal. Some argue that it must be a Muslim who carries out the slaughter, but some quote the Qu'ran 5:5 as meaning that People of the Book can also carry this out provided it is done according to the rules. True Halal meat should be prepared using these rules. Unfortunately, if some videos circulated online are true, not all meat sold as Halal has been correctly slaughtered by these rules.

All pork is forbidden to Muslims as is the consumption of alcohol. Meat from animals that have 'died of themselves' is forbidden, presumably because it might be diseased. The Hadith also carries further prohibitions against donkey meat, predatory animals with fangs or canine teeth such as dogs, cats lions etc., birds with talons, lizards, snakes, scorpions and vermin. Also barred are eels, crows, apes, horses and mules.

Space for reader's notes

Space for reader's notes

20 – Marriage (and divorce)

Customs vary from one community to another with regard to the marriage ceremony, but all have in common witnesses and a contract detailing the dowry. This varies with the social practice and the standing of those involved, but it is constant throughout Islam, as it is a price paid to the father of the bride for marital rights. Usually, only part payment is made at the wedding, the residue having to be paid if the marriage ends in divorce. The terms of this civil contract can permit the bride to keep control of her dowry and other property, and may also include that she shall be her husband's only wife and add the right to later divorce. All very businesslike.

This is purely a civil style of contract without religious overtones such as apply to a church wedding between Christians. Males may marry "People of the Book", that is Christians and Jews, but not polytheists, that is those that have a belief in more than one God. Muslim women may only marry Muslims. Although marriage is not a religious sacrament, the Qur'an is firm in its doctrine that the foundation of marriage is mutual love, trust, concern and fidelity, in much the same way as marriage is regarded in Christian tradition. Both husband and wife are responsible for the family home and for care of the children. The husband's roles are to protect the home and the family, to set policies and priorities, but he should not be unkind, insensitive and despotic. A husband and wife should be as close as "each other's garments" (Qur'an 2:183). As the Prophet Muhammad said, "The best among you is he who treats best the members of his family." The wife's roles are to see to the comfort and welfare of her husband and children, to be faithful to him, to take care of his possessions and bring "warmth, joy and peace" to the home.

Islam allows divorce but it is strongly discouraged, and in the Hadith, the Prophet Muhammad is quoted as saying, "The most obnoxious act in the sight of God is divorce." There are extensive measures for mediation and reconciliation, every effort is made to avoid the break up of the marriage. If this cannot be avoided, then set procedures have to be followed. A wife being divorced by her husband is granted a waiting period or idda during which time she must be cared for. This is to be certain she is not pregnant. After this, she is allowed to remarry. If she is pregnant, the idda is extended so that she is cared for until after the child is born. Traditionally, divorce was done by the husband, declaring three times in front of witnesses, "I divorce you". Some countries now have a legal divorce through their courts which treat men and women equally. Custody goes automatically to the mother for children under nine for girls and under seven for boys, but after those ages the children can choose which parent they want   to live with.

It can be seen that the role of the Muslim man is different from that of the woman because of his gender, but this should not be seen as indicating superiority. The roles of male and female are regarded as being complementary without one being above the other. Each takes the lead role in differing aspects of life, the man as provider and protector, the woman as mother and home builder. The Qur'an commands both to be virtuous and modest in their behaviour and dress. A woman must not undermine the credibility of her decency by immodest clothing, nor risk the arousal of sexual desire in other men by dressing in such a manner. (Qur'an 24:31) Rules of morality are very stringent and breaches of these roundly condemned. These rules of dress and modesty seem very strict, harsh even, by some western standards where they may be seen as oppressive, but in Islamic thinking they are there to protect women. After all, even in the west, in olden days a glimpse of stocking was looked on as something shocking.

In the next chapter, the customs surrounding and the significance of death will be discussed.

Space for reader's notes

Space for reader's notes

21 – Death

Westerners are mostly familiar with the image of the white Taj Mahal. Perhaps fewer know that it is a memorial containing a tomb and was constructed by about 20,000 workers from 1631 to 1648 in Agra in northern India by the Emperor Shah Jahan to house the tomb of his favourite wife, Mumtaz Mahal. The massive domed structure was constructed using white marble and inlaid gems. At each corner is a minaret, and passages from the Qur'an adorn the outside walls. The bodies of the emperor and his wife remain in a vault below the building. It must be said of course that most Muslims do not have such lavish burial places.

Most people will have seen on television the funeral processions of Muslims, accompanied by crowds of wailing women in a manner that is disconcerting to westerners. But this wailing is part of the Muslim customs surrounding death, and continues from the death until burial. This time is mercifully short because of the origins of Islam in a hot desert climate. While the women wail, the deceased is washed in water, by a member of the same sex, and the burial shroud put on. The body is carried to the cemetery by men taking turns, while those in the procession chant the Muslim profession of faith, "There is no god but God, and Muhammad is His messenger." There are prayers of praise to God and invocations of blessings on Muhammad.

The deceased is placed in the grave lying on his or her right side facing Mecca. While the grave is filled, a prayer from the first chapter of the Qur'an is recited.

A gravestone is not usually erected as this is against strict Islamic teaching, but in practice, graves are often marked, from the simple wooden markers we are so painfully familiar with from Bosnia through to Syria, up to huge monuments such as the Taj Mahal. The graves of Muslims who died in the world wars fighting with the Allies often have simple headstones in military cemeteries. These have sometimes been attacked in recent years by radical Islamists, a notable case occurring in Libya where the headstones of non Muslim soldiers were vandalised, causing outrage in the west, and also it must be said, among many Muslims in Libya.

After death, two angels, Munkar and Nakir arrive to question the deceased on their religion. If they respond correctly, they are shown their place in Paradise, and then told to sleep peacefully until the Day of Resurrection. Unbelievers and sinners, however, are beaten, shown their place in Hell and left with their grave pressing upon them until the end of days.

Life after death is spiritual rather than physical, and its nature is beyond human understanding. In Islam life on this earth and one's response to it, the doing of God's will in this life, is far more important than hoping for eternity, because one will be judged on one's actions in this life. Belief in life after death and belief in the one God are unified - to deny one is to deny the other.

Space for reader's notes

Space for reader's notes

22 – *Jerusalem, calendars and festivals*

The city of Jerusalem lies at the heart of the three main Abrahamic religions, Judaism, Christianity and Islam. At the heart of this ancient city is the site of the great Jewish temple which Jews believe was built by King Solomon of Israel and Judah, and later rebuilt as the Second Temple of Jewish tradition in the sixth century BC (BCE) and which was destroyed by the Romans in 70AD (70 CE) to crush a Jewish revolt. Many Jews believe that a third temple will be built on the site, known as Temple Mount. One wall of the ancient temple supporting structure remains which is a site of great holiness for Jews and is known as the Wailing Wall because there Jews mourn the destruction of their temples. Christians of course regard Jerusalem as the Holy City because it was the site of the crucifixion, burial and resurrection of Jesus Christ. Mercifully not from the Temple Mount as that would only further complicate things, although of course Christ visited the temple. For Muslims, Jerusalem and specifically the Temple Mount is of great significance because that is from where the Prophet Muhammad is believed to have made his night journey to heaven. The magnificent Dome of the Rock mosque with its distinctive golden dome now stands on the Temple Mount site of the Jewish temples along with the Al-Aqsa Mosque which means "the Farthest Mosque" and which is the third holiest site in Islam.

With all these competing claims and the reverence in which the city is held, and especially the Temple Mount by Jews and Muslims, it is little wonder that the question of who governs Jerusalem and who has access to these holy places is one the world's most intractable problems and the major barrier to peace in the middle east and between Islam and Judaism.

A Muslim festival directly associated with the Prophet Muhammad is that of Lailat al-Miraj or the night journey. This holds that during one night, the Prophet Muhammad was taken from Mecca to Jerusalem in a white winged chariot and thence to heaven where he met earlier prophets, (including Jesus) and God himself. He then returned to Mecca. This is based mainly on Hadith or the Tradition, and a short passage in the Qur'an. Dante's Inferno draws on this. The site of the ascent is marked by the Dome of the Rock on the Temple Mount. Muslims originally prayed towards Jerusalem until God instructed the Prophet Muhammad to turn to the Kaaba in Mecca instead.

Most people are aware that the Islamic Calendar is different from that used in the west. This is so because as described above the Islamic year is lunar rather than solar, and has 354 days, divided into twelve months, but not the same months as in the western calendar. Because of this the Islamic year moves back through seasons. There is no easy equivalent western date for any Islamic date because the 'day' runs from sunset to sunset rather than midnight to midnight. There have also been variations of the Islamic calendar in different parts of the Islamic world which has led to some confusion. Whilst it is retained for religious purposes, in many places it is now used for other matters in conjunction with the western solar calendar which makes life simpler in the modern world for travel and business etc. Conversion from one calendar to another involves a lengthy calculation but thankfully a computer or smartphone can make short work of the complicated formula involved in conversion.

The best known month to westerners is probably the ninth, Ramadan, which is a time of fasting (see chapter 17). A major festival is observed at the end of this time, Id al-Fitr. This lasts for three or four days at the beginning of the tenth month, and is a time of joy and the giving of alms to the poor. It is a time of prayer and rejoicing, for dressing up and exchanging gifts, particularly of sweets etc. after the fasting, much as in the west much chocolate is eaten at Easter after the supposed deprivations of Lent.

A major festival celebrated in connection with the pilgrimage, the Hajj, is Azha. This is when Muslims remember the story of Abraham's sacrifice of a sheep instead of his son. This feast can last up to four days in some countries. Every Muslim is expected to sacrifice an animal that they can afford, and where possible by strict Islamic slaughter methods. The animal is then cooked and given to the family, neighbours and the poor in three equal parts. The exchange of gifts also takes place at this time. It is a traditional time to visit the graves of relatives for prayer.

The New Year (Muharram, which is also the name of the first month) lasts for up to ten days, particularly for Shi'ites for whom it also has significance as a time of mourning for the death of Hussein (see chapter 11). Sunni Muslims concentrate on the Creation, which is said to have occurred on this day.

The birthday of the Prophet Muhammad on the twelfth day of the Islamic month of Rabi' al-awwal is also celebrated widely (Shi'ites celebrate it on the seventeenth day). As this is an Islamic date, it changes each year on the western calendar. Even though this is about the birth of the Prophet, many Muslims oppose this birthday celebration as it smacks of idolatry. Only God is worthy of worship, and to some, the celebrations of Muhammad's birthday comes close to crossing that line.

There are many other Islamic festivals, differing from one area to another, locally based and often centred around local shrines and events. One such is the Shi'ite gathering at Karbala in modern Iraq where the Prophet's grandson, Hussein ibn Ali, was killed.

23 – Islam and Christianity

As we draw near the end of this little book, it is perhaps time to look at Islam in relation to other faiths, Christianity in particular. Obvious differences have become apparent during the book, as well as the common roots and shared traditions of the faiths. No short chapter such as this can hope to do more than simply highlight these. The controversy that has raged between Islam and Christianity for centuries cannot easily be summarised.

Muslims do not accept the Jewish and Christian scriptures as westerners do because they are seen as tradition, not the Word of God, which is only manifest in the Holy Qur'an. This is the only definitive statement of God's word, the final correction of all that had gone before.

Muslims reject the concept of God the Father, because in their eyes this diminishes God, ascribing a physical relationship to man which is to them repulsive. Even in a metaphorical sense, it is rejected because men are not God's children, but His servants and creatures.

The notion of Trinity is also abhorrent to Islam (see chapter 2). This is seen as an attempt to associate other entities with God who alone is infinite, absolute and omnipresent. The Qur'an makes a special appeal to Christians, the People of the

Book, to serve none but God and to connect none with Him. (3:57) This clear distinction between God and everything else in the universe and all other creatures means that the Christian view of Jesus is to Islam, indefensible. Jesus, with His clear place of birth and a birth date, contradicts the infinity and absoluteness of God. To attempt to associate the physical and temporal with God is an unpardonable sin. To Muslims, the Christian concept of God the Father, God the Son and God the Holy Spirit, the Trinity, is almost polytheism, the worship of multiple gods.

As far as Muslims are concerned, Jesus of Nazareth cannot be divine, as seen above. He is however regarded as one of a line of prophets whose task may have been divine, but who were themselves simply human, including Jesus. Among the prophets, Jesus has a special position, second only perhaps to the Prophet Muhammad. He is regarded as a great teacher, the Messiah of the Jews, whose assignment from God was to bring the Jewish people back to the right path from which they had strayed, and also to bring the whole of humanity back from the worship of idols and the worship of false gods. The Virgin Birth is seen as a sign of prophethood, not divinity, and Mary is on a par with Khadijah and Fatima, the Prophet Muhammad's wife and daughter, in the esteem of Islam. Jesus's message of humility, justice, love, charity, compassion, purity and truth is accepted by Islam.

The differences between the world's two major religions continue in the next chapter.

Space for reader's notes

Space for reader's notes

24 – Original Sin and the truth of scripture

The doctrine of Original Sin is one which Christian theologians and thinkers have discussed and argued about for centuries, and not all Christians accept it. Islam has no such problem - the notion is completely rejected. The idea that man has some kind of inherited sinfulness is rejected on the basis that God would not have created such an imperfect creature. As far as Islam is concerned, sin is simply the disobedience to the will of God. Sin as a concept does not concern Islam, but what does matter are the actions of man, either obedient or disobedient to God's commands; these are the real concern. Islam has no absolute standard of what is right and wrong apart from this. To have such a standard apart from what is the will of God would be to recognize another source of authority alongside God – and that is unthinkable.

The Genesis story of the Garden of Eden makes no symbolic points about the intrinsic sinfulness of man. The eating from the Tree of Knowledge was an act of disobedience of God for which forgiveness was sought and was given. According to the Prophet Muhammad, man is born pure and innocent. Whether he then obeys the commands of God thereafter is up to him, and he is responsible for his own actions.

In a way in Islam there is a 'points system'. For everything you do, you either get a good mark or a bad mark, which will be calculated during Resurrection Day. Those with more good deeds than bad will go to Heaven, and those with more bad deeds than good will go to Hell. Therefore, fasting on certain days of the month / of the week will give extra points for the Muslim. The deed system works basically like this:

Wajib: This means a certain deed is mandatory and there is no excuse for not doing it. Leaving it will mean a bad mark and doing it will mean a good mark. Examples are fasting during Ramadan, prayers etc.

Sunat: This means a certain deed is preferred - if you don't do it, no harm, but you get extra points if you do. An example is fasting on certain days as discussed before.

Haram: This means a certain deed is a no-no. Doing it means a bad mark and leaving it means a good mark. Examples are adultery and unjustified crime.

Makruh: These are the deeds that are not encouraged for you to do, but it will not get you a bad mark if you do. An example is smoking.

Harus: These are normal deeds, like getting married, eating and stuff like that. Like a catch all for the rest that does not go into any of the above.

The Holy Qur'an is regarded as the true word of God, given to one person over twenty-three years and contemporaneously recorded. This is in marked contrast to the Bible of the Jews and Christians which is a collection of stories, with many different authors, mostly unidentified or unverified, spread across thousands of years, during such time the message of God they were supposed to pass on has been distorted, either by the passage of time and errors of memory, or intentionally by men for their own purposes. (See chapter 6) The same applies to the four Gospels. Muslims find it hard to understand that there can be four Gospels, which undermines the reliability of any of them. How can they all be true? Many Muslims believe that the real Word of God was brought by Jesus but was then lost, and that the four Gospels were written later in an attempt to replace that. However, this does not matter because the real message of God was given again to the Prophet Muhammad and that is preserved in the Holy Qur'an. Many in Islam misunderstand Christian theological debate, which is seen as Christians actually doubting their own faith, and in their minds this strengthens their belief in the unreliability of the Bible and the truth of the Qur'an. Christianity is seen as doubting itself in contrast to the certainty of Islamic belief which comes directly from God. Educated Islamic scholars are naturally more aware of the nuances of analysis which Christian theologians discuss at such length.

Thus, although Jews and Christians share much common tradition with Muslims, and have a unique place in Islam as "People of the Book", (see chapter 10) there are significant and apparently irreconcilable differences. It is a great pity for us all that these differences so often overshadow the common message of peace, justice and equality.

Space for reader's notes

25 - *Islam in the modern world*

I hope that over the past two dozen chapters, some of the misconceptions about Islam have been dispelled. Islam has had a high profile in recent years because of the involvement of some of its adherents in radical political movements which have ranged across the world, from Palestinian liberation and the establishment of Islamic Law in some countries to the Black Power movement in the United States. On top of this of course are the actions of a comparatively small number of Muslims who adhere to what the vast majority would say is a distorted and radical interpretation of Islam leading to the murderous atrocities of the 9/11 attacks and many more such as the barbarity of the so-called Islamic State.

Islam, like much in the modern world, is going through a period of change and flux. Some traditionalists fear the influence of western ideas which they view as secular, over materialistic and corrupting. In contrast progressives would like to see Islam take on the challenges of the modern world. Conflict both within and without Islam is the result. Much of the traditional influence in Islam comes from the Shi'ites. These are a small minority within Islam as a whole but they wield considerable influence through various religious and political movements they control, especially helped by the Islamic

Republic of Iran, where Shi'ites form the overwhelming majority. The mainly Sunni Arab states therefore view Iran with suspicion, while at the same time accepting there is the common Islamic faith. Yet even within Shi'ite Iran, and elsewhere in the Islamic world, there are progressive thinkers who argue that Islam and democracy are not only compatible but indispensable to each other. They argue that to be a true Muslim one must be free because enforced faith is no faith at all. Both religious and political empowerment of the people are as important as each other therefore in the true Islamic state, where the will of the people would lead to both political freedom and the acceptance of Islam.

As in medieval Christianity where all scripture and litany was in Latin, the power of the clergy, especially in the Mullah led Shi'ite states, depends on the control of information. The increasing global flow of information and the trouble governments have controlling this, especially through the use of satellite technology and electronic communication such as the Internet mean that the democratisation of Islam is likely to happen, but no doubt there will be an increasingly bitter struggle on the way, both among the various factions within Islam and also between Islam and the outside as the battle is fought over the coming decades. This is a factor governments the world over will need to take into account.

In compiling this book, I have of course used my own knowledge, but obviously on many occasions have had to refer to other sources for verification and to research points on which I was not sure. I have used many sources to do this, but for those wishing to know more, a principle and valuable book which lent its structure to this little book is "Islam, the Way of Submission", by Solomon Nigosian of Toronto University. When I first did my research Microsoft Encarta was a valuable resource, (and that shows how long ago that was!). Now of course the Internet and the World Wide Web has yielded both facts and comment. Not forgetting both the Holy Bible and Holy Qur'an which both have been sources of reference. For those who wish to take their inquiry into Islam further, any of these is a good place to start.

I hope you have found this little book interesting, and that it has given you a greater understanding of Islam.

Space for reader's notes

Space for reader's notes

Appendix 1 The 99 Names of God

1. Allah (The God)
2. Al 'Adl (The Just)
3. Al 'Afuw (The Pardoner)
4. Al Ahad (The Nondivisible)
5. Al Akhir (The Final)
6. Al Ali (The Most High)
7. Al Alim (The Learned)
8. Al Awwal (The First)
9. Al-Azim (The Greatest)
10. Al Aziz (The Most Mighty)
11. Al Badi (The Introducer)
12. Al Ba'ith (The Ressurector)
13. Al Bari (The Manifestor)
14. Al Barr (The Benevolent)
15. Al Basir (The Perceiving)
16. Al Basit (The Expander)
17. Al Batin (The Transcendental)
18. Dhu al Jalal wa al Ikram (Having Majesty And Splendour)
19. Al-Fatir (The Inventor)
20. Al Fattah (The Judge)
21. Al Ghaffar (The Oft Forgiving)
22. Al Ghafur (The Most Forgiving)
23. Al-Ghalib (The Victor)
24. Al Ghani (The Bounteous)
25. Al Hadi (The Leading)
26. Al Hafiz (The Preserver)
27. Al Hakam (The Intercessor)
28. Al Hakim (The Knowledgeable)
29. Al Halim (The Patient)
30. Al Hamid (The Praiseworthy)
31. Al Haqq (The Sincere)
32. Al Hasib (The Calculating)
33. Al Hayy (The Eternal-living)

34. Al Jabbar (The Strongest)
35. Al Jalil (The Dignified)
36. Al Jami' (The Cumulator)
37. Al Kabir (The Grandest)
38. Al Karim (The Generous)
39. Al Khabir (The All-Aware)
40. Al Khafid (The Demeaning)
41. Al Khaliq (The Maker)
42. Al Latif (The Kind)
43. Al Majid (The Glorious)
44. Al Malik (The King)
45. Malik al Mulk (The Guardian Of Empowerment)
46. Mani' (The Withhelding)
47. Al Matin (The Steadfast)
48. Al-Mawla (The Supporter)
49. Al Mu'akhkhir (The Delayer)
50. Al Mubdi (The Initiator)
51. Al Mughni (The Blesser)
52. Al Muhaimin (The Protector)
53. Al Muhsi (The Accounter)
54. Al Muhyi (The Lifegiver)
55. Al Mu'id (The Reinstater)
56. Mu'izz (The Honorgiving)
57. Al Mujib (The Responsive)
58. Al Mu'min (The Faithgiving)
59. Al Mumit (The Deathbringer)
60. Al Muntaqim (The Retaliator)
61. Al Muqaddim (The Promoter)
62. Al Muqit (The Coordinator)
63. Al Muqsit (The Equitable)
64. Al Muqtadir (The Controller)
65. Al Musawwir (The Proportioner)
66. Al Muta'ali (The Supreme Highness)
67. Al Mutakabbir (The Magnificent)
68. An-Nasir (The Keeper)
69. An Nur (The Light)
70. Al Qabid (The Straightener)

71. Al Qadir (The Competent)
72. Al Qahhar (The Subduer)
73. Al-Qarib (The Near)
74. Al Qawi (The Nontiring)
75. Al Qayum (The Self-Reliant)
76. Al Quddus (The Holiest)
77. Ar-Rabb (The Lord)
78. Ar Rafi' (The Uplifting)
79. Ar Rahim (The Merciful)
80. Ar Rahman (The Beneficient)
81. Ar Raqib (The Watchful)
82. Ar Ra'uf (The Considerate)
83. Ar Razzaq (The Providing)
84. Al Sabur (The Forbearing, The Patient)
85. As Salam (The Source Of Serenity)
86. As Samad (The Eternal)
87. Al Sami (The Aware)
88. Ash Shahid (The Watcher)
89. Ash Shakur (The Indebting)
90. At Tawwaab (The Magnanimous)
91. Al Wadud (The Affectionate)
92. Al Wahhab (The Rewarder)
93. Al Wahid (The Singularity)
94. Al Wajid (The Considerer)
95. Al Wakil (The Trustee)
96. Al Wali (The Patron)
97. Al Waarith (The Succeder)
98. Al Wasi' (The Vast)
99. Az Zahir (The Apparent)

Space for reader's notes

Appendix 2 Also by Patrick C Notchtree

Maxym: He looks like an angel but kills like a devil.

Growing up in a Russia plagued by homophobia, Maxym wrestles with his conflicting emotions towards Muslims and his own suppressed homosexuality. Alongside his innate psychopathic tendencies and an unsettling fascination with killing, his exceptional marksmanship skills make him a coveted asset. Trained to be an unrelenting assassin, he walks a precarious tightrope, embodying a paradoxical blend of tender affections and unwavering loyalty to the nation that nurtured him—an enigmatic figure in the tapestry of contemporary Russia.

Maxym's insatiable thirst for revenge propels him into perilous missions across Syria, Africa, Iraq, Libya, and Afghanistan, amassing immense wealth at a young age. However, the year 2022 brings with it a reckoning in Ukraine, demanding an exorbitant price for his actions. Amidst the tangled web of Maxym's journey lies a poignant exploration of the intricate bond between Ukraine and Russia. The stifling atmosphere of Putin's Russia forces him to conceal his true sexual identity, facing mounting danger as time progresses. Inspired by true events, this gripping tale unravels the extraordinary life of a young Russian, set against the backdrop of a 21st-century ordinary Russian family. This biographical novel delves deep into the human psyche, exploring themes of love, loyalty, and the relentless pursuit of justice

Available for Kindle, audio and in Paperback

Not suitable for under 18s or the faint-hearted

http://www.maxym.net/

"The Clouds Still Hang" - a biographical memoir of the author's life. Available in large print and as an audiobook.
www.thecloudsstillhang.com

"Apostrophe Catastrophe" – which explains why there is just one simple rule for the apostrophe, as well as some other 'grammatical grumbles'.

"Hunting Harry", a little novella. An inheritance of millions awaits, but the will contains some rather awkward stipulations. So how to get round those?
http://www.limebury.com/users/notchtree/index.htm#harry

Index

Space for reader's notes

Space for reader's notes

Space for reader's notes